PORTRAIT OF
WESTCOUNTRY RACING

FIONA CRAWFORD

Best wishes
Fiona Crawford.

HALSGROVE

First published in Great Britain in 2008

Copyright © Fiona Crawford 2008
www.fionacrawford.co.uk

British Library Cataloguing-in-Publication Data
A CIP record for this title is available from the British Library

ISBN 978 1 84114 798 7

HALSGROVE
Halsgrove House,
Ryelands Industrial Estate,
Bagley Road, Wellington, Somerset TA21 9PZ
Tel: 01823 653777 Fax: 01823 216796
email: sales@halsgrove.com
website: www.halsgrove.com

Printed and bound by Grafiche Flaminia, Italy

ACKNOWLEDGEMENTS

I dedicate this book to my biggest fans, my husband and my father.

There are too many people to mention who have helped me with this book but you all know who you are; all the racecourse staff and race goers, lads, lasses, trainers and owners who have all allowed me to photograph and quiz them without hesitation. My only regret is that not all the photographs could make it into the final cut.

Last of all a huge apology to all my family and friends who must have thought I had been abducted by aliens as I have been off the radar for the six months I have dedicated to this book.

INTRODUCTION

This book is just a small collection of some of the characters I have come across since starting this project: truly a portrait of Westcountry National Hunt racing.

I have had a fantastic six months travelling around the South West National Hunt racecourses at Exeter, Newton Abbot, Taunton and Wincanton. Everyone I have met has been engaging and helpful. This book hopefully reflects that, as well as all the excitment of attending the race meets.

I was lucky enough to spend time at a couple of training yards. Colin Heard's yard which is recently established in Cornwall and David Pipe's well established and reputable yard in Somerset.

To complement the training and racing I headed to John and Sarah Haydon's breeding yard in Devon to see where the whole process starts.

3rd June, East Burrow Farm, Devon
Double Trigger

Double Trigger was one of the highest individual Group winners. He was undefeated as a 2 year old showing outstanding speed, a Classic Winning 3yo and Classic placed Cartier Champion European stayer at 4 years. After his successful career on the track ***Double Trigger*** retired to John and Sarah Haydon's stud at East Burrow Farm in Devon in 1999 where his success has carried on with his progeny. This includes having sired 23 winners under NH rules including such names as ***Twelve Paces***, ***Trigger The Light***, ***Presumptious***, ***Earlsfield Raider***, ***Major Comet***, ***Sun Pageant***, ***Russian Trigger***, ***Brikies Mate***, ***Aye***, ***Pairtree***, ***Angies Double***, ***Gold Reef***, ***Charmaine Wood***, and ***Double Magnum***.

3rd June, East Burrow Farm, Devon
John Haydon dishing out afternoon feeds for the mares.

Opposite:
3rd June, East Burrow Farm, Devon
The mare is **Double Flyte** and the foal is by the stallion **And Beyond**.
The foals are not named until they are purchased to race.

7th May, East Burrow Farm, Devon
The mare is *Tulipa* and her foal is by *Generous*.

Opposite:
7th May, East Burrow Farm, Devon
The foal in the foreground is out of *New Dawn* by the stallion
Overbury and the mare in the background is called *Blessed*.

7th May, East Burrow Farm, Devon
The mare is *Solway Rose* and her foal is by *Gentleman's Deal*.

7th May, East Burrow Farm, Devon
A field of East Burrow Farm-owned mares and foals.

3rd June, East Burrow Farm, Devon
One of **Double Trigger's** foals
out of the mare **Linden Grace**.

Opposite:
3rd June, East Burrow Farm, Devon
This nosey yearling is out of
Free Spirit by the stallion **Dr Fong**.

3rd June, East Burrow Farm, Devon
This yearling is out of *Royal Dream* by *Needwood Blade*.

3rd June, East Burrow Farm, Devon

Top right: Chestnut yearling is by **Best of the Bests** and out of **Blessed**, the bay is also by **Best of The Bests** out of **Miller Maid**.

Bottom right: Left to right; **Millar Maid** yearling, **Blessed** yearling and **Royal Dream** yearling.

Bottom left: Left to right: **Millar Maid** yearling, **Blessed** yearling and **Royal Dream** yearling.

3rd June, East Burrow Farm, Devon
Double Trigger. 'Give an inch and he will take a mile…' Sarah Haydon.

16th April, Boscastle, Cornwall
Trainer Colin Heard and his wife Karyn on their gallops, riding *River Heights* and *Classic Rarity* respectively.

16th April, Boscastle, Cornwall

The gallops. Colin's father Brian Heard (also a point to point and pony race rider in his youth) prepares the gallops every day ready for Karyn and Colin to start exercising. The yard is an old dairy farm and lends itself well to the recent conversion to a training yard. The only training yard in Cornwall to race under rules (at National Hunt racecourses) that I could find.

16th April, Boscastle, Cornwall
Colin and Karyn do all the work themselves but have an excellent support team in the form of family and friends. When I visited they had 6 horses in training, both point to pointers and National Hunt horse. They are hoping to increase that number for next season.

27th April, Newton Abbot Racecourse, Devon 7.45pm
The Teign Suite Novices' Hunters' Steeple Chase (Class 6). *Innocent Rebel*, trained by Colin Heard, wins his first race under jockey Nick Scholfield for owner Mrs Caroline Wilson.

Colin and Karyn lead *Innocent Rebel* and Nick Scholfield into the winner's enclosure.

Karyn offering *Innocent Rebel* a drink.

Mr Gary Wilson, Nick Scholfield, *Innocent Rebel*, Karyn Heard and owner Mrs Caroline Wilson.

16th April, Boscastle, Cornwall
Innocent Rebel and Colin at home. Although Colin and Karyn were really busy when I visited I was made very welcome and they were generous with their time and input. They make the biggest mugs of tea too!

19th March, Exeter Racecourse

19th March, Exeter Racecourse

19th March, Exeter Racecourse

Top: Mending hurdles. *Above:* (left to right) Vic Newman, Mike Curtis, David Northam and Jim Stokes.

29th February, Taunton Racecourse

Jockeys' Changing Room.

Peg ready for Robert 'Chocolate' Thornton.

Declarations boards.

Jockeys' Changing Room.

29th February, Taunton Racecourse

29th February, Taunton Racecourse

The racecourse stables with St Michael's church in the background.

The ground staff treading in. Post race preparations are all done in the days after a race meet ready for the next one. (Left to right) Kevin Coucill (Estate Manager), Grant Reed, Ken Bestford, Simon Garrett, Davis Lunniss, Fly, Fred Diamond, Bryn Bowler and Tony Smith.

Terrie Scott is the Stable Manager, in charge of the 90 stables at Taunton Racecourse. Pictured here with Holly. Terrie owns the racehorse *Misskurimoon*, who is in training with Miss M Bragg in Buckfastleigh.

9th April, Newton Abbot Racecourse
Jason Loosemore (Estate Manager) and Scott Duff moving a hurdle fence for the next race meet.
Hurdles are moved regularly to keep the ground fresh and give the best running for the horses.

9th April, Newton Abbot Racecourse
Jason Loosemore (left), Stuart Ranson (front right) and Scott Duff (back right).

9th April, Newton Abbot Racecourse
Jason Loosemore trimming the hurdle.

Opposite:
9th April, Newton Abbot Racecourse
Scott and Stuart carrying in the wings.

19th March, Exeter Racecourse
Saddlecloths in the Weighing-in Room.

JOCKEYS ARE REMINDED IT IS THEIR RESPONSIBILITY TO WALK THE COURSE, READ THE MAP AND INSTRUCTIONS IN THE WEIGHING ROOM PRIOR TO THE DAY'S RACING

19th March, Exeter Racecourse
Jockeys' Changing Room.

6th March, Wincanton Racecourse

Moreen Conway selling the *Racing Post* at Wincanton. Moreen and husband Mike have been selling the *Racing Post* at Wincanton, Exeter and Newton Abbot for about 23 years. They used to cover 11 racecourses but since semi-retirement they do just the three Westcountry racecourses and help out at Salisbury and Cheltenham when needed.

28th February, Taunton Racecourse

No ticket – no entry – Taunton's friendly bouncer, Bernard Bulley. Bernard is part of a much larger network of retired boys who provide casual labour on race days. From stewarding to ground staff, the roles change depending on the course. I get the feeling they do it for the love of it rather than the money. They all enjoy the social side as well as the horses plus the chance to place a few bets.

3rd April, Taunton Racecourse
3.30pm The DH Payne & Son Maiden Hurdle Race (Class 4). No 13, *My Nicole* in the Parade Ring pre-race.

22nd March, Newton Abbot Racecourse

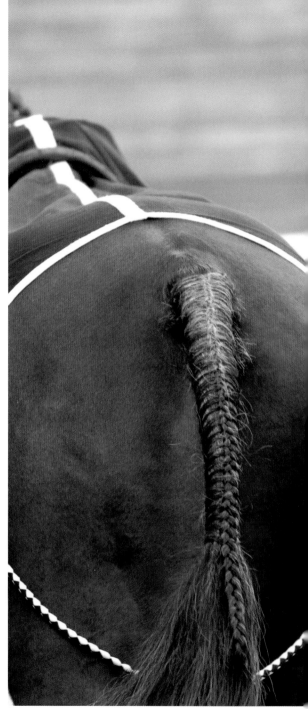

17th June, Newton Abbot Racecourse
7.15pm The 24th June is Ladies Night Maiden Hurdle Race (Class 4).
Wise Men Say being led round the Parade Ring.

10th February, Exeter Racecourse
2.00pm The Toteplacepot Handicap Hurdle Race (Class 3). *Stumped* (no 2) being led round the Parade Ring.

Opposite:
13th May, Newton Abbot Racecourse
7.10pm The Teign Novices' Steeple Chase (Class 4). Ruby Walsh and A.P. McCoy
lead out the jockeys; Ruby Walsh went on to win the race on *Poquelin*.

22nd March, Newton Abbot Racecourse

Brian Stanely, one of the Parade Ring Stewards gets ready to ring the bell to summon the jockeys to mount.

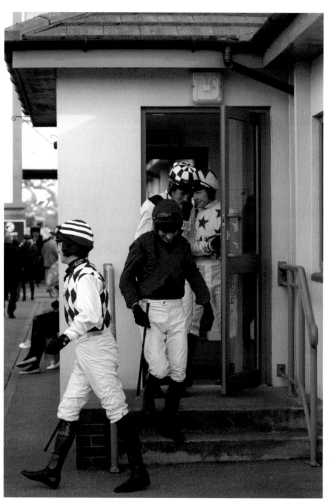

Jockeys being called out.

5th June, Newton Abbot Racecourse
2.30pm The Newton Abbot Racecourse Lady Riders' Selling Handicap Hurdle Race (Class5).
The lady jockeys entering the paddock.

17th June, Newton Abbot Racecourse
8.15pm The Happy Birthday Sean Dooner Handicap
Hurdle Race (Class 3). Tom Malone being led out
onto the course on *Soliya*.

17th June, Newton Abbot Racecourse
7.45pm The Kingsteignton Handicap Steeple Chase
(Class 5). Mr D. Cook on *River Dante* being led
out by Linda Blackford – former area point to point
champion jockey, now turned trainer.

5th June, Newton Abbot Racecourse
5.00pm The Car Boot Sale Here 29th June Handicap
Hurdle Race (Class 4). Richard Johnson sharing the joke,
on *Talkingstick* to finish 3rd. Leaders, right Bob Vallender,
left Heddwyn Edwards.

30th January, Exeter Racecourse
2.20pm The Sponsor A Race Here At Exeter Handicap Hurdle Race (Class 4). Timmy Murphy on *Boulevardofdreams* going to the start.

13th November, Exeter Racecourse
3.05pm The WBX.Com 0% Commission On Big Races Beginners' Steeple Chase (Class 3). Sam Thomas takes *Ouninpohja* to the start.

17th June, Newton Abbot Racecourse
8.45pm The River Teign Classified Steeple Chase (Class 5). A.P. McCoy on *Charge It* being led out onto the course, goes on to finish 2nd.

10th February, Exeter Racecourse
2.00pm The toteplacepot Handicap Hurdle Race (Class 3). Gerard Tumelty on *Silencio* make their way to the start.

22nd March,
Newton Abbot Racecourse
4.05pm Southwest Racing Club
Handicap Hurdle Race (Class 4)
Dave Crosse on *Federstar*.
going to the start.

30th January, Exeter Racecourse
2.50pm The Exeter Handicap Steeple Chase (Class 4). (Left to right) Daryl Jacob on *Macmar* (to finish 1st), Timmy Murphy on *Alcatras*, Tom Scudamore on *Nacadour* (to finish 2nd), Joe Tizzard on *Ironside* and Simon Elliot on *Supreme Tadgh*.

27th March, Exeter Racecourse

3.55pm The City Of Exeter Challenge Cup Novices' Steeple Chase (Class 3). Joe Tizzard on **Bay Mouse** having some final adjustments made to the girth by the start team before the off. **Bay Mouse** has come into his racing career from British Eventing. Many a good racehorse has gone on from the track to make a good event horse. **Bay Mouse** has done this the other way round, he has competed at British Eventing Intro, Pre Novice and Novice Level from 2005 to 2007 under Emma and Harriet Nuttall. Bred by A. E. S. and Mrs Nuttall and owned by Mr Nuttall, it is a true family affair. **Bay Mouse** is trained by Colin Tizzard in Dorset. **Bay Mouse** didn't win here at Exeter but went on the win at Newton Abbot on the 9th June 2008.

7th February, Taunton Racecourse
2.20pm The Somerset Local Medical Committee Maiden Hurdle Race (Class 4).

Above: **7th January, Taunton Racecourse**
1.40pm The 3rd Battalion The Royal Welsh Novices' Hurdle Race (Class 3).
The field with St Michael's church in the background. **Group Captain** (Colours –
royal blue and yellow stripes and checked sleeves – mid field in photograph)
went on to win this race under the guidance of Robert Thornton.

Right: **5th January, Wincanton Racecourse**
1.10pm The Higos Insurance Somerton Novices' Handicap Hurdle Race (Class 4).
The field on the final bend before the run in to finish. **Mous Of Men** went on to win
under G. Lee (leader in photograph, far left of frame, emerald green spots on white cap),
Miss Midnight with A. Coleman came in 2nd (black and white hooped cap).

9th June, Newton Abbot Racecourse
3.30pm The Happy Birthday Nicola Monaghan 30 Years Young Novices' Hurdle Race (Class 3).
The Hon. Mrs Townshend's **Woolcombe Folly** with A. P. McCoy (middle, black cap) pulls through to win while
Johnny Bissett with A. Coleman on board came in second (right, light blue cap). **Orvita** and Owyn Nelmes (left, dark and light blue quartered cap) finished 4th. **Woolcombe Folly** is trained by Paul Nicholls at his yard in Shepton Mallet.

7th December, Exeter Racecourse
2.10pm The Axminster Carpets Devon Marathon Handicap Steeple Chase (Class 3). My competition!

5th January, Wincanton Racecourse
12.40pm The Higos Direct Novices' Hurdle Race (Class 4) (Div 1).

17th June, Newton Abbot Racecourse
8.15pm The Happy Birthday Sean Dooner Handicap Hurdle Race (Class 3).
Tom Malone on *Soliya* (left) and R. Greene on *Bobsleigh* (right).

30th January, Exeter Racecourse
Some of the raceday ground staff. From left to right: Basil Townsend, Reg Slater, Valentine Mills, Mike Fren, John Fleet and Bob Clampett. Familiar faces – all these boys work at the other racecourses in the region, each time with different roles and responsibilities.

7th December, Exeter Racecourse
Treading-in on a wet day.

5th January, Wincanton Racecourse
Nigel Payne clearing the water jump of fallen birch.
Notice the blue dye that makes the water a distinctive colour.

3.10 The Country Gentlemen's Association Steeple Chase
(A Limited Handicap) (Class 1) (Listed Race). Left to right: *Naunton Brook* with David England, *Neptune Collonges* with Liam Heard and *Preacher Boy* with James White. The race was won by *Neptune Collonges*, who later went on to come third in the Cheltenham Gold Cup Chase, giving the south-west trainer Paul Nicholls his 1,2,3 in the race. *Denman* 1st, *Kauto Star* 2nd and *Neptune Collonges* 3rd. *Naunton Brook* came in 2nd and went on to run in the Grand National. Whilst *Preacher Boy* did not complete this race he also went to the Cheltenham Festival to come 4th in the Golden Miller Trophy.

3.10 The Country Gentlemen's Association Steeple Chase
(A Limited Handicap) (Class 1) (Listed Race). Far side *Naunton Brook* and near side *Neptune Collonges* on their last circuit of the track.

3.40pm The Bathwick Tyres Kingwell Hurdle Race (Class 1) (Grade 2)
Katchit and Robert Thornton clear the last hurdle to go on to win. This same combination
went to the Cheltenham Festival and won the Champion Hurdle Challenge Trophy. *Katchit*
is owned by the D S J P Partnership and trained at Barbury Castle by Alan King.

16th February, Wincanton Racecourse
The Country Gentlemen's Association Steeple Chase Trophy
– this year going to **Neptune Collonges**.

16th February, Wincanton Racecourse
The Bathwick Tyres Kingwell Trophy – this year going to Katchit.

30th January, Exeter Racecourse
The Assistant Manager Vicki Robinson asking the winning owners
to come forward and collect their prize.

31st January, Wincanton Racecourse
Jeff Payne and Geoff Udall preparing the start tape.

6th May, Exeter Racecourse
Linda Humphries (left) and Jean Foster (right), part of the St John's Ambulance team who have provided invaluable first-aid care on racedays at Exeter since 1940. Sadly they have collectively decided they can longer provide cover and their last race meet was the 14th May 2008.

10th February, Exeter Racecourse
2.30pm The toteexacta Novices' Hurdle Race (Class 1) (Listed Race).
Coming out onto the track to start. Front row from left to right: Chris Honour on *Stagehand* (beige and maroon,) Dominic Elsworth on *Luxurix* (light and dark blue), Noel Fehily on *Laredo Sound* (red and dark blue) and Joe Tizzard on *Archie Gunn* (dark green and red).

10th February, Exeter Racecourse

2.30pm The toteexacta Novices' Hurdle Race (Class 1) (Listed Race).

Stagehand and **Laredo Sound** get the lead at the start. **Group Captain** won the race with Robert 'Choc' Thornton (blue and yellow checked sleeves) pictured here at the back of the field.

18th March, Exeter Racecourse
4.20pm. The Robert Webb Travel Open Hunters' Steeple Chase (Class 5).
Miss R. Green on **Gaye Trigger**.

25th April, Newton Abbot Racecourse
5.35pm The River Teign Handicap Hurdle Race (Class 4).
The field just after the off.

29th January, Taunton Racecourse
2.40pm The Orchard Restaurant Beginners' Steeple Chase (Class 4).

29th January, Taunton Racecourse
4.10pm The Deane Veterinary Centre Handicap Steeple Chase (Class 3).
Left to right – Daryl Jacob on *Malaga Boy*, Kevin Tobin on *Alphabetical* and Paul Moloney on *Brave Villa*.

30th January, Exeter Racecourse
2.50pm The Exeter Handicap Steeple Chase (Class 4).
An unfortunate fall for Liam Heard on *Classic Fair*. Liam demonstrates the perfect jockey fall position. The horses all jumped over him, *Classic Fair* got to his feet to finish and Liam walked home with no damage apart from maybe his pride!

10th October, Exeter Racecourse
3.50pm The Dean & Dyball Handicap Steeple Chase (Class 4).
On the left, **September Moon** (bred by H.M. The Queen) and Byron Moorcroft went on to be placed 3rd even after this awkward landing at the last; on the right, **Sky Warrior** was not so lucky and fell here with Christian Williams on board.

5th June, Newton Abbot Racecourse

Right:
5th January, Wincanton Racecourse
12.40pm The Higos Direct Novices' Hurdle Race (Class 4) (Div 1).
The field passing the bookies first time round.

30th January, Exeter Racecourse
4.20pm The Come Racing Here On February 10th Handicap Hurdle Race (Class 5).
Winning jockey Mr J. Barnes on Mr Berwick's ***Mungo Jerry*** exchanges some banter
with trainer David Pipe as they pass.

25th April, Newton Abbot Racecourse
5.35pm The River Teign Handicap Hurdle Race (Class 4).
Buckfastleigh-based trainer Jimmy Frost celebrates with one of the
winning connections of *Critical Stage*.

14th May, Exeter Racecourse
3.20pm The Exeter Racecourse Intermediate Hunters' Steeple Chase (Series Final) (Class 4).
Polly Gundry goes on to win with *Kiama*, Polly looking over her shoulder to see the rest of the field chasing up behind.
Kiama is trained by Polly Gundry at her Axminster yard, and owned by Mrs Vickery.

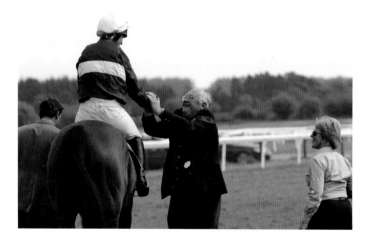

14th May, Exeter Racecourse
3.20pm The Exeter Racecourse Intermediate Hunters' Steeple Chase (Series Final) (Class 4).
The thrilled connections.

14th May, Exeter Racecourse
3.20pm The Exeter Racecourse Intermediate Hunters' Steeple Chase (Series Final) (Class 4). Polly Gundry being interviewed by Richard Pitman the well-known TV commentator and former top jump jockey.

6th March, Wincanton Racecourse
3.25pm The Betfredcasino Handicap Hurdle Race (Class 4).
The Weighing-in Room. Left Joe Tizzard, 3rd in this race with *Rudivale* and
P.J. Brennan on the scales for Clerk of the Scales Georgina Roberts.

18th March,
Exeter Racecourse
Mel Baskwill, part of the starting team; if there is a false start Mel raises the flag, if not then Mel runs.

30th January, Exeter Racecourse
2.50pm The Exeter Handicap Steeple Chase (Class 4).
Waiting for the start.

18th March, Exeter Racecourse
2.50pm The canadatravelcentre.co.uk Novices' Handicap Hurdle Race (Class 4).
Left to right: *Marghub* and T. J. Phelan (dark blue and grey), the winner *Push The Port* and Jay Pemberton (pink and royal blue), *Zaffarella* and Felix de Giles (red and black spots) and Ted Moss with *Willie McCarthy* (orange and black).

18th March, Exeter Racecourse
3.20pm The Elizabeth Finn trust Novices' Steeple Chase (Class 3).
Keepthedreamalive with Daryl Jacob over the second from last to finish fourth.

3rd April, Taunton Racecourse
2.55pm The South Tetcott Hunt Supporters Novices' Steeple Chase.
Leading Attraction (white and black spots) and Liam Heard have the advantage on this final fence but finish 2nd, **Menchikov** (mauve and pink check) is in third place here with Mick Fitzgerald but they pull through to win.

Opposite:
13th May 2008, Newton Abbot Racecourse
6.10pm The Paddock Restaurant Mares Only Novices' Hurdle Race (Class 4).
Aimigayle and Colin Bolger fly the final fence to finish fourth.

27th March, Exeter Racecourse
2.50pm The Desert Orchid Restaurant Handicap Hurdle Race (Class 3).
Richard Johnson (no 3) on *Or Bleu* battles it out with Liam Heard on **Purple Patch** to take first and second respectively.

Opposite:
10th February, Exeter Racecourse
4.05pm The totecourse to course Novices' Steeple Chase (Class 3).

10th October, Exeter Racecourse
2.20pm The Dean & Dyball Conditional Jockeys' Selling Handicap Hurdle Race (Class 5).
Winner Harry Skelton on *Temper Lad*, owned and trained by Jimmy Frost.

30th January, Exeter Racecourse
4.20pm The Come Racing Here on February 10th
Handicap Hurdle Race (Class 5).
After the race – time to cool down.

Left:
13th May, Newton Abbot Racecourse
6.40pm The Newton Abbot Racecourse
Selling Hurdle Race (Race 5).
Winner *Kosciusko* getting a dowsing
in the winner's enclosure.

13th April,
Newton Abbot Racecourse
Ivor Brimblecombe – a familiar voice at Newton Abbot, Exeter and Taunton Racecourse for the past 54 years. Ivor is the announcer for colour and weight changes, non runners and the results. His most important announcement on race day is 'Horses Away, Horses Away, Weighed In, Weighed In', which signals to everyone that all the jockeys from the race have been weighted in by the Clerk of the Scales and that the result of the race has been confirmed. Bookies can then pay out to the lucky punters and the winning connections can really start to celebrate.

19th May, Newton Abbot Racecourse
John Wonnacott – one of the race day staff.

31st January, Wincanton Racecourse

31st January, Wincanton Racecourse

7th January,
Taunton Racecourse
One of the viewing towers
used by race day officials.

95

30th January, Exeter Racecourse
One of the casual staff taking a break between races.

29th January, Taunton Racecourse
Removing the hurdle in the back straight ready for the final race of the day, The National Hunt Flat Race.

28th February, Taunton Racecourse
John Hills, the Managing Director of Taunton Racecourse.

Opposite:
28th February, Taunton Racecourse
2.30pm The southwest-racing.com Selling Handicap Hurdle Race (Class 5)
Can Can Flyer in the parade ring. He went on to be placed 3rd in this race.

99

30th January, Exeter Racecourse
4.20pm The Come Racing Here on February 10th Handicap Hurdle Race (Class 5).
No 8, **Prince Bere** and Tom Scudamore and no 15, **Chagiz** and Simon Elliott go out onto the track before the start.

7th December, Exeter Racecourse
2.10pm The Axminster Carpets Devon Marathon Handicap Steeple Chase (Class 3).

David Dennis and *The Risky Viking* go over the last to win, owned by the syndicate Gale Force Two and trained by Nick Williams from his South Molton yard.

T.J. O'Brien came in third on *Amazing Valour*.

3rd April, Taunton Racecourse

4.40pm The southwest-racing.com Handicap Hurdle Race (Class 4). The field just after the start.

Opposite:

7th January, Taunton Racecourse

2.40pm The Thoroughbred Breeders' Association Golf Day Mares Only Maiden Hurdle Race (Class 4). The field.

7th February, Taunton Racecourse
2.50pm The Somerset Local Medical Committee Maiden Hurdle Race (Class 4) (Div II).
No 5, Sam Thomas on *Pacha D'oudairies*, no 1, Liam Heard on *Bold Policy*, no 4, Liam Treadwell
on *Noble Future* and no 3, Tom O'Connor on *First Friend*.

10th February, Exeter Racecourse
3.30pm The totesport 0800 221 221 Handicap Steeple Chase (Class 3).
The Sawyer and W. Kennedy taking on a chase fence to finish 2nd.

6th May, Exeter Racecourse
5.50pm The Farmers Friend of Exeter Maiden Hurdle Race (Class 4). A close battle for the finish, ***Nothing Is Forever*** and Noel Fehily (dark blue and red) made it with ***Alaghiraar*** and Jack Doyle (dark green) taking second, ***High Standard*** and P. Brennan (dark blue and white) and ***Cornish Jester*** and Chris Honour (maroon and beige) follow on.

Opposite:
3rd April, Taunton Racecourse
2.55pm The South Tetcott Hunt Supporters Novices' Steeple Chase (Class 4).
Jockeys Keiran Burke and Harry Skelton watch the race unfold.

30th January, Exeter Racecourse
3.50pm The Exeter Racecourse Conference Centre Handicap Steeple Chase (Class 4).
The corner leading into the back straight. Left to right: *Eluvaparty* with R. Greene (yellow and dark blue)
finished 3rd, *Josear* with Chris Honour (grey and maroon) finished 4th, *WhatcanIsay* with Richard Johnson
(royal blue and white) finished 2nd and *Nemetan* with Christian Williams (pinks, on the right) went on to win.

25th April, Newton Abbot Racecourse
8.05pm The Paddock Restaurant Standard National Hunt Flat Race (Class 6).
First time past the stands. Left to right: ***Puerto Azul*** with J. Quintin (blue and pink), ***Misskurimoon***
with Paul Callaghan (pink and black) and ***Green Belt Elite*** with C. Thompson (red and blue) the
only one to be placed coming in to finish 3rd. ***Misskurimoon*** is owned by Terrie Scott,
Taunton Racecourse Stable Manager.

10th February, Exeter Racecourse
2.30pm The toteexacta Novices' Hurdle Race (Class 1) (Listed Race). *Working Title* with Mick Fitzgerald (yellow and purple) battle with Richard Johnson on *Overclear* for 2nd place. *Working Title* took 2nd and *Overclear* came across the line in 3rd.

6th May, Exeter Racecourse
5.50pm The Farmers Friend of Exeter Maiden Hurdle Race (Class 4).
The final hurdle. Left to right: *Simondiun* with R. Walsh (dark blue and grey), *Cornish Jester* and Chris Honour (maroon and beige), *Alaghiraar* and Jack Doyle (dark green), *High Standard* and P. Brennan (dark blue and white).

**2nd May,
Newton Abbot Racecourse**
Finding the perfect pitch.

Opposite:
**27th March,
Exeter Racecourse**
The bookies.

3rd April, Taunton Racecourse
4.40pm The southwest-racing.com Handicap Hurdle Race (Class 4).
Tom Siddall on *Great Tsar*.

10th October, Exeter Racecourse
4.20pm The Nash Dash Handicap Hurdle Race (Race 4).
Winner **Marronnier** with Keiran Burke clear the last in style. Finishing in 4th place was **Milford Lescribaa**
with Tom Scudamore (back left) and 3rd place went to **King Kasyapa** with T. O'Brien (back right).

17th June, Newton Abbot Racecourse
A busy evening meet.

5th June,
Newton Abbot Racecourse
Summer jump racing
brings in the crowds.

29th January, Taunton Racecourse
Getting out of the elements between
races for the ground staff.

5th January, Wincanton Racecourse
Anyone for golf? Geoff Udall practicing his
swing in between races. Wincanton Racecourse
has a 9 hole golf course in the centre of the track,
obviously for non race days!

28th February, Taunton Racecourse
The resident race day cars ready for the off.

9th June, Newton Abbot Racecourse
4.30pm The Racecourse For Your Corporate Event Handicap Hurdle Race (Class 4).
Natoumba is urged on to the finish under Richard Johnson to come a final 3rd.

19th May, Newton Abbot Racecourse
The 25th May, Car Boot Standard Open National Hunt Flat Race (Class 6).
A winner for owner Mrs Findlay and Minehead-based trainer Philip Hobbs with *Canaradzo* under Richard Johnson (purple and grey) in the lead from the first circuit, *Tigger* with Gerry Supple sitting on his shoulder (maroon and yellow stars). *Saffron Spring* with Claire Stretton (dark green and dark blue), *Wade Farm Billy* with Jamie Moore (royal blue and black) and *C'monthehammers* with P. Brennan (maroon and light blue) sit comfortably in behind.

121

19th March, Exeter Racecourse

Opposite:
27th March, Exeter Racecourse
2.20pm The Exeter Novices' Selling Hurdle Race (Class 5). The field.

18th March, Exeter Racecourse
2.50pm The canadatravelcentre.co.uk Novices' Handicap Hurdle Race (Class 4).
The field passing the crowd on the first circuit.

6th November, Exeter Racecourse

At 850ft they say that Exeter Racecourse is the highest racecourse in the land and the second longest at 2 miles. I think they should add to this claim that it is the coldest!

13th April, Newton Abbot Racecourse
2.20pm The Racing Here 25th April Maiden Hurdle Race (Class 4) (Div II).
The field on the first circuit. Front row left to right: *Freddy's Start* and Matty Roe (red and white)
and *Moncada Way* with Richard Johnson (black and white check).

Opposite:
5th January, Wincanton Racecourse
3.25pm The Higos Insurance Services Handicap Steeple Chase (Class 3).
Mort De Rire and Andrew Thornton make their way to the start.
They came in 4th for the Blandford-based Alner training yard.

5th January, Wincanton Racecourse
3.55pm The Higos Direct Novices' Hurdle Race (Class 4) (Div II).
A winner for Miss H. Knight with **Quarry Town** under jockey G. Lee.

10th February, Exeter Racecourse
3.00pm The totesport.com Graduation Steeple Chase (Class 2).
Dream Alliance and Richard Johnson lead the field over the water jump on the first circuit.

16th February, Wincanton Racecourse
4.50pm The Bathwick Tyres Dorchester Handicap Hurdle Race (Class 4).
The field head off into the fast-setting sun in the last race of the day.

The last rider coming in to finish.

10th June, Nicholashayne, Somerset
David Pipe and *Comply or Die* at the Pipe yard.

Left:
13th April, Newton Abbot Racecourse
David Johnson's *Comply or Die*, the 2008 John Smith's Grand National winner parading at Newton Abbot just 9 days after his big win at Aintree. *Comply or Die* is trained by David Pipe at his Somerset yard.

10th June, Nicholashayne, Somerset
Comply or Die, enjoying his summer holiday.

10th June, Nicholashayne, Somerset
The string heading onto the gallops.

Left:
10th June, Nicholashayne, Somerset
Collecting together before heading out onto the gallops.

This page and opposite:
10th June, Nicholashayne, Somerset
The gallops.

10th June, Nicholashayne, Somerset

Opposite:
10th June, Nicholashayne, Somerset
A quick debrief for David Pipe and his jockeys before they head up the gallops for the second time.

 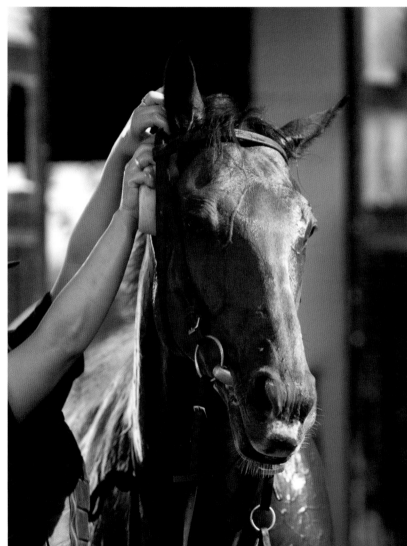

10th June, Nicholashayne, Somerset
A well-earned hose down and *Wise Owl* enjoying a wash down.

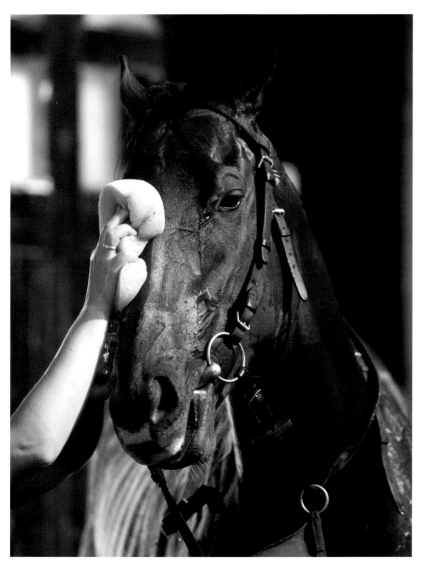

10th June, Nicholashayne, Somerset
One Nation taking his turn in the pool. Emma Carrow is in the centre of the pool and Sue Lower is on the outer edge.
They use a swing bridge to get backwards and forwards so the horse can do several laps without stopping.

10th June, Nicholashayne, Somerset
One Nation taking a dip.

10th June, Nicholashayne, Somerset
The walk home.